Human Rights

and the

US Drug War

A treatise on the United Nations
Universal Declaration of Human Rights
and the US Bill of Rights

By Chris Conrad, Mikki Norris
and Virginia Resner

Creative Xpressions • California, USA • 2001

Human Rights and the US Drug War

Adapted from the Human Rights and the Drug War exhibit project, also known as Human Rights 95 (HR 95).

Visit the Human Rights and the Drug War web page:
http://www.HR95.org

Acknowledgements:
Agape Foundation, Amnesty International, Eleanor Roosevelt, Family Council on Drug Awareness, Families Against Mandatory Minimums, Human Rights Watch, the United Nations, the prisoners and their families and all those working for social justice.

For more information write to:
PO Box 1716, El Cerrito, CA 94530 USA
www.chrisconrad.com
To arrange an exhibit, call 510-215-8326
Email: Mikki@hr95.org

ISBN 0-9639754-5-5

Published by Creative Xpressions, El Cerrito CA.
Printed and bound in the USA by Central Plains Printing.

Published by Creative Xpressions
PO Box 1716, El Cerrito, CA 94530 USA • www.chrisconrad.com

Contents

The United Nations Charter
Article 1.3

Purposes and Principles. To achieve international co-operation in solving international problems of an economic, social, cultural, or humanitarian character, and in promoting and encouraging respect for human rights and for fundamental freedoms for all without distinction as to race, sex, language, or religion.

UN Universal Declaration of Human Rights

Preamble: *Whereas* recognition of the inherent dignity and of the equal and inalienable rights of all members of the human family is the foundation of the freedom, justice and peace in the world. ...

Whereas disregard and contempt for human rights have resulted in barbarous acts which have outraged the conscience of mankind, . . .

Now, therefore The General Assembly proclaims this Universal Declaration of Human Rights

Article 29.2

In the exercise of his rights and freedoms, everyone shall be subject only to such limitations as are determined by law solely for the purpose of securing due recognition and respect for the rights and freedoms of others and of meeting the just requirements of morality, public order and the general welfare in a democratic society.

Introduction to Human Rights and the US Drug War

It is time for Americans to reassess our policies.

The General Assembly of the United Nations proclaimed the *UN Universal Declaration of Human Rights* (UDHR) in 1948 as a global response to the Nazi Holocaust. Based on the United States' *Bill of Rights*, this document enumerates for all people a broad spectrum of economic, cultural, political and civil rights.

Its Preamble states, "The General Assembly proclaims this Universal Declaration of Human Rights as a common standard of achievement for all peoples and all nations, to the end that every individual and every organ of society, keeping this Declaration constantly in mind, shall strive by teaching and education to promote respect for these rights and freedoms and by progressive measures, national and international, to secure their universal and effective recognition and observance."

The UDHR is not directly enforceable; however, many of its principles are written into legally binding treaties (see page 67).

---

*Almost 60% of federal prisoners are
behind bars for drug offenses;
Only about 3% are for violent offenses.*

A stated goal of international human rights law is to achieve mutual tolerance. By contrast, America's drug policy is termed "zero tolerance." This is significant. Begun as a moralistic crusade against a demonized population on the wrong side of the somewhat arbitrary line drawn between legal and illegal drugs, the Drug War has evolved into a massive, profit-driven industry that thrives on the doctrine of prohibition.

In the past 30 years, the US has gone from being "The Land of the Free" to one of the world's biggest prison states.

The US reached 2,000,000 prisoners in the year 2000. It incarcerates more of its citizens than any other developed nation. Over 400,000 drug offenders are behind bars nationally, and the number is growing. Almost two-thirds of federal prisoners are charged with drug activities that were not even illegal at the beginning of the Twentieth century.

The Human Rights and the Drug War exhibit project demonstrates that the US government is currently committing human rights violations against its own people. In the name of the Drug War, subcultures are demonized and scapegoated. Families are torn apart. Children are orphaned. Women are the fastest growing population in prison. African Americans are disproportionately targeted, largely due to disparities in sentencing and the concentration of law enforcement personnel in inner city areas. The Drug War not only violates international law, but the US Constitution as well. Every year, more of our rights are taken away and harsher penalties are enacted to send a message about being 'tough on drugs.' It's time to examine the effect these policies have on the rights of all Americans.

Our objectives are to increase awareness of human rights and the *Universal Declaration of Human Rights*; to promote mutual respect and tolerance; and to advocate for a peaceful solution to the Drug War. Our goal is to bring drug policy into compliance with international human rights law and the US Constitution.

This book was originally prepared to commemorate the 50th Anniversary of the UDHR. It is even more relevant today than it was in 1998. It identifies violations of human rights in America and illustrates them through personal stories. The cases presented here are a small but representative sample of the thousands of untold stories of the people serving time for non-violent drug offenses. This is intended to alert the international human rights and political communities about the social harm that the Drug War and prison industry is inflicting on American freedoms.

This book is not about drugs. It is about injustice. It is about reviving human rights.

— Chris Conrad, Mikki Norris and Virginia Resner
Creators of HR 95, Human Rights and the Drug War

1. Undermining Due Process

The rule of law is based on the premise of equality, justice and "the whole truth."

The phrase "due process of law" refers to the course of legal proceedings established by a nation or state to protect individual rights and liberties. In the United States, the structure of due process is enshrined in the Bill of Rights — the first ten Amendments to the US Constitution. Statutory laws enacted by elected legislative bodies must comply with the Constitution.

Courts must apply the Constitution to ensure fair application of justice, and they have the authority to strike down unconstitutional laws. Unfortunately, this system of checks and balances has been eroded by the Drug War. This is a pattern that is commonly known as the "drug exception" to the Bill of Rights.

Before a person gives legal testimony, they are required under penalty of perjury to swear to tell "the truth, the whole truth, and nothing but the truth." Yet there are many things the jury is not allowed to know and the judge is not allowed to consider. Even grand juries directed to look into drug cases and hand down indictments are kept in the dark about circumstances and evidence that could affect their decisions.

Due process and the courts are our ultimate defense against injustice and bad laws. Sentencing guidelines and mandatory minimum penalties tie judges' hands to prevent them from using discretion in drug cases. They must only look at the type and quantity of drugs involved and the defendant's criminal history, rather than consider the mitigating circumstances and individual characteristics of the person charged.

The prosecutor determines what charges are leveled, and thus the penalties. Prosecutorial threats, secret informants and back room plea bargains have replaced public hearings and the search for justice amid "the whole truth."

UN Universal Declaration of Human Rights
Article 10
Everyone is entitled in full equality to a fair and public hearing by an independent and impartial tribunal, in the determination of his rights and obligations and of any criminal charge against him.

Article 11.1
Everyone charged with a penal offense has the right to be presumed innocent until proved guilty according to the law in a public trial at which he has had all the guarantees necessary for his defense.

United States Constitution / Bill of Rights
Fifth Amendment
No person shall be held to answer for a capital, or otherwise infamous crime, unless on a presentment or indictment of a Grand Jury, except in cases arising in the land or naval forces, or in the Militia, when in actual service in time of War or public danger; nor shall any person be subject for the same offense to be twice put in jeopardy of life or limb; nor shall be compelled in any criminal case to be a witness against himself, nor be deprived of life, liberty, or property, without due process of law; nor shall private property be taken for public use without just compensation.

Sixth Amendment
In all criminal prosecutions, the accused shall enjoy the right to a speedy and public trial, by an impartial jury of the State and district wherein the crime shall have been committed, which district shall have been previously ascertained by law, and to be informed of the nature and cause of the accusation; to be confronted with the witnesses against him; to have compulsory process for obtaining witnesses in his favor, and to have the Assistance of Counsel for his defense.

Under civil asset forfeiture law, a person's entire life savings can be seized or frozen (but not forfeited) before they are even charged with a crime, let alone convicted. When all your money is gone, you cannot hire a good attorney to defend yourself.

The competence of judge and defense counsel have a direct bearing on court rulings that establish the defense, include or exclude evidence, and determine what the jury is allowed to hear. Medical necessity and religious use arguments are frequently disallowed in drug cases, thus limiting a person's defense strategies and a jury's access to truth. Juries are not informed of the penalty which a defendant faces, nor of their own power to acquit in the interest of justice, despite the evidence.

Conspiracy law allows people who have never even touched drugs or money to be prosecuted in the Drug War. Physical evidence has been supplanted by hearsay. Each person is held fully responsible for the entire offense, no matter how small or insignificant their role was. It is not even necessary for a crime to be committed to implicate you in a conspiracy. Talking about breaking a drug law is enough ... even hearing someone mention the idea in your presence. This is different than in normal criminal law, where proof is required that a crime occurred or an overt act was taken towards committing a crime.

Witnesses in drug cases are enticed by prosecutors to provide "substantial assistance." They are offered a chance to reduce or work off their own charges if they provide possible evidence against others. Informants (anonymous or identified) are paid to give evidence, which can lead to perjured testimony.

Police entrap people to break the law or increase quantities of sales to enhance penalties. They also seize personal property for law enforcement use. One scandal in the Los Angeles Ramparts Division revealed police stealing drugs and money, planting evidence and falsifying testimony that affected at least 800 cases. Other scandals have rocked New York City and elsewhere.

The Drug War is the pretext used to round up, and lock away for unduly long periods of time, many people who are minor participants in drug offenses — or who may even be innocent.

The net effect of all this is to undermine due process of law.

Amy Ralston Pofahl

*sentenced to
24 years*

*Amy received a
Presidential Clemency,
after serving 9 years in
prison*

*charged with conspiracy
to import and distribute
ecstasy*

Amy Ralston's husband was Charles "Sandy" Pofahl, a successful Dallas businessman and graduate of Stanford Law School. They were married for a few years, then separated due to his alcohol problem. In 1989, they had been apart for a year. Amy owned Prime Time, a promotional company in Los Angeles.

Her nightmare began when she learned that her estranged husband had been arrested for manufacturing and distributing ecstasy (MDMA) in Germany. He mistakenly thought ecstasy was legal there at the time. Some was traced to the US.

Amy helped Sandy arrange his finances during his trial and early confinement. As a result, she was targeted by prosecutors. "Federal agents promised that if I refused to help them gain the information against my husband, they would destroy my life. This they did," recalls Amy. Her friends and clients were intimidated by agents who said Amy was a drug dealer and just associating with her would get people into trouble.

Amy was arrested and charged with money laundering; but also with conspiracy to commit all the crimes attributed to her former husband and his co-defendants. She refused to plea bargain or 'cooperate' by fabricating information. Her court-appointed attorney misled her and refused to present evidence and witnesses she requested and needed. Her trial was moved to a Texas court reputed to have a 100% conviction rate. Sandy was convicted, got a six year sentence in Germany and was released in four. Amy was sentenced to 24-years in a US prison for *his* crimes.

Glamour magazine featured Amy's story

Amy continued to work tirelessly on her own behalf. Her story drew international attention and was featured on *Court TV*, in *Glamour* magazine, and in the book *Shattered Lives: Portraits From America's Drug War*. Human Rights and the Drug War organized a "Free Amy" campaign to focus on her case.

She spent over nine years in prison — her entire thirties behind bars. After exhausting all her appeals, her only hope was executive clemency. On July 7, 2000, Amy walked free; one of only five non-violent drug offenders given clemency that day by President Bill Clinton after more than seven years in office. He granted several more clemencies during his final days in office.

"It was a bittersweet victory," said Amy, reflecting on the many thousands of other drug offenders whose harsh sentences continue to shatter their lives and families. "Why only five?"

Amy has dropped her ex-husband's surname. She is working to put her life back in order and to advocate for justice for others.

Women are the fastest growing population in prison. Over 75% of women in prison are mothers.

Since federal mandatory minimum sentences were enacted in 1987, the number of women inmates has tripled. The majority of these women are first-time, non-violent, low-level offenders.

Conspiracy law implicates many women in drug cases by association with husbands or boyfriends.

Danielle Metz

serving three Life sentences plus 20 years

a mother charged with her husband's cocaine conspiracy

Danielle, left, with her children

Debbie Mendes

serving 12 years, 7 months

Bookkeeper charged with her employer's cocaine conspiracy

Debbie, right, kneeling, with her daughter

Melinda George

serving 99 years

charged with sale of 1/10th gram of cocaine

State of Texas penalty

Melinda, left.

Hamedah
Ali Hasan

*sentenced to
LIFE without
parole, reduced
on appeal to 12
to 27 years*

**Hamedah, with head
covering, and children**

*charged with conspiracy to distribute cocaine / base, interstate travel
in the aid of racketeering, use of a telephone to commit a felony*

Hamedah Ali Hasan's instructors attest that she was an impressive student with lots of promise, poised to make a decent life for herself and her three daughters. She felt she was ready to turn her life around and seek employment with her exceptional skills. Unfortunately, she never got the chance.

Instead, her life was turned upside down by the police, and she now sits in prison with a life sentence for a crime she says she did not commit. Hamedah had no prior criminal or arrest history. She was never seen doing anything illegal related to the offenses for which she was convicted.

Shortly after her arrest, she was offered immunity (all charges dropped) in exchange for her 'cooperation' with the US Attorney to obtain a conviction against her cousin. She had no knowledge of the offenses and refused to lie for the 'deal.' As a result she got a harsher penalty. The prosecution consisted primarily of hearsay testimony from people who directly benefitted, either by getting immunity themselves or, if they were already in prison, in exchange for a possible sentence reduction.

"Experience has clearly shown me that almost any violation of the law is excusable as long as the accused 'cooperates' with government attorneys and/or officials," wrote Hamedah.

Her youngest daughter was born in prison.

Memorial at the site
where 18-year old
Esequiel Hernandez
was shot dead by
US Marines who
were patrolling the
border area for
drugs. See story on
page 16.

Photo by
James Evans.

UN Universal Declaration of Human Rights

Article 3

Everyone has the right to life, liberty and security of person.

United States Declaration of Independence

We hold these truths to be self-evident, that all men are created equal, that they are endowed by their Creator with certain unalienable Rights, that among these are Life, Liberty and the pursuit of Happiness. That to secure these rights, Governments are instituted among Men, deriving their just powers from the consent of the governed. That whenever any Form of Government becomes destructive of these ends, it is the Right of the People to alter or to abolish it, and to institute new Government, laying its foundation on such principles and organizing its powers in such form, as to them shall deem most likely to effect their Safety and Happiness.

2. The Right to Life

In memory of the civilian casualties of the Drug War

The foremost human right is the right to one's life, from which all other rights spring. Killing innocent civilians is not acceptable in war, and should never be a component of domestic police policy; but it happens in the US Drug War.

Part of the problem is the government's zeal to use no-knock raids and excessive force to seize evidence and round up drug suspects. When civilians are hurt or killed, the subsequent investigation routinely states that no one was at fault. We cannot overlook or forget the human fatalities of the Drug War.

- **Rev. Accelyne Williams** (MA), 75, died of a heart attack when drug enforcement police forcibly entered the wrong apartment and chased him around his home until he collapsed.

- **Shirley Dorsey** (CA) was driven to commit suicide in 1991 rather than testify against her boyfriend, who was growing medical marijuana for her use to control chronic pain.

- **Gary Shepherd** (KY) was a Vietnam veteran shot to death in 1993 for growing marijuana — assassinated by concealed snipers while he stood with his family on his front porch.

- **Annie Rae Dixon** (TX), 84, a grandmother, was shot to death in her sick bed during a 1992 no-knock search.

- **Alberto Sepulveda** (CA) was only 11 years old when he was killed in 2000 by a police officer, as the little boy was waking up and getting out of bed. A joint operation of DEA, FBI and local police had raided his home and were arresting his father on federal drug charges when this tragedy happened.

- **Chad MacDonald** (CA) was a minor threatened with a lengthy jail sentence for methamphetamine when police offered him a deal to entrap dealers. In 1998, on his fourth setup, Chad went into a suspected drug house, where he was exposed as an informant, then tortured and killed.

• **Patrick Dorismond** (NY), 26, a security guard and father of two, was standing outside a bar when he was approached by an undercover agent trying to set up a "buy and bust" in March, 2000. When the agent asked where he could buy some marijuana, Dorismond told him to get away from him. A scuffle ensued and the undercover agent called for his partner who was waiting nearby for help. Dorismond was quickly shot and killed.

• **Ismael Mena**, (CO), 45, was shot and killed in 1999 by a team of a few SWAT agents who entered his home on a no-knock search warrant. Not knowing who the armed intruders were, Mena pulled a gun in self-defense, and pointed at the agents, who shot and killed him. It turned out that the paid informant gave police the wrong address. No drugs were found in his home.

• **Mario Paz** (CA), 65, was a grandfather asleep with his wife when police officers shot the locks off his doors and stormed into his bedroom in 1999 looking for marijuana. Officers claimed he was reaching for a gun when they shot him in the back, which the family denies. The search warrant did not identify Paz as a suspect — it named a former neighbor who occasionally used their address to receive mail.

Preventable Deaths

In 1995, HIV infection became the leading cause of death among persons aged 25 to 44 years.

According to the Centers for Disease Control, by year-end 1999 there were 733,374 reported cases of AIDS in the US. Of these, 263,789 – 35% – are linked to injection drug use.

In 1998, the Secretary of Health and Human Services reported that, "A meticulous review has now proven that needle exchange programs can reduce the transmission of HIV and save lives without losing ground in the battle against illegal drugs."

In 2001, federal law still interferes with needle exchange.

Source: **www.DrugWarFacts.org**. Common Sense for Drug Policy

Donald Scott

Died in 1992 at age 62

*Shot in his own home by a
Drug Task Force*

	I CERTIFY THAT IN MY OPINION DEATH OCCURRED THE HOUR, DATE AND PLACE STATED FROM THE C... STATED.	
CORONER'S USE ONLY	29. MANNER OF DEATH—specify one: natural, accident, suicide, homicide, pending investigation or could not be determined. HOMICIDE	30A. PLACE OF INJURY Residence

Donald Scott was a Malibu, CA, millionaire who owned 250 acres of breathtaking ranch land adjacent to federal parklands. Attempts had been made by the government to buy the property, but Scott was not interested in selling it. On October 2, 1992, Scott and his wife, Frances Plante, were awakened by a loud pounding at the front door of their house.

As Plante attempted to open the door, a narcotics task force from the LA County Sheriff's Department burst into their home, weapons loaded and in hand. She was pushed forcefully from the door at gun point and cried out, "Don't shoot me, don't kill me!" With a gun aimed at her head, Plante saw her husband run into the room, waving a revolver above his head. She heard a deputy shout, "Put the gun down! Put the gun down! Put the gun down!"

As Scott lowered his gun, three shots rang out, apparently from two sources. Her husband was killed instantly. The coroner listed the cause of death as a "homicide."

Claims that there might be pot growing on the land, made by agents who did aerial surveillance, were used to get a search warrant. No marijuana was found in their home or grounds. Scott, 62, did not even smoke it.

An official inquiry and report by Ventura County District Attorney Michael Bradbury suggested that agents were motivated by the expectation that this raid would lead to forfeiture of the Scott property. His family eventually received $5 million from the taxpayers as a wrongful death settlement.

Esequiel Hernandez

Died in 1997 at age 18

Shot to death by US Marines

First US citizen killed by military troops on US soil since 1970, when students were shot by National Guard troops at a Vietnam War protest at Kent State University, Ohio.

Esequiel 'Zeke' Hernandez was one of the "best and brightest" of Redford TX, an isolated border town with a population of nearly 100. Before his death at age 18, he held aspirations of becoming a game warden or park ranger.

Prior to Reagan's administration, the Posse Comitatus Act prevented military troops from engaging in domestic law enforcement. It was amended to accommodate the Drug War.

Townspeople had no idea that Marines were patrolling the area wearing 'ghillie suits' that make them virtually invisible. Zeke was tending his family goat herd when he was shot by a 22-year-old Marine Corporal who was part of Joint Task Force Six, a military unit assigned to anti-drug operations. The camouflaged Marines were hiding in the bushes looking for drug smugglers.

While tending the herd, Zeke carried a rifle to protect his goats from snakes and wild animals. The Marines claim he fired twice in their direction before one of them fired the fatal shot from an M-16. Townspeople say they heard only one single gunshot. The autopsy showed that Esequiel was not facing the Marine who killed him. He lay on the ground bleeding and unattended for 20 minutes before he died.

The government has not cleared Zeke of wrongdoing or apologized to his family. The Marine, however, was cleared in 1998 and no charges were ever filed against him. Zeke's family filed a wrongful death suit against the government and won $1.9 million in damages. But money cannot replace Zeke's life and unrealized potential, which were cut short by the Drug War.

Jared Lowry

Died in 1997 at age 21

Death due to preventable medical complications after a heroin overdose

Jared Lowry's troubles began during a spring break trip with friends living near Houston, TX, when he was arrested at the age of 17 for a small amount of marijuana. Though he was prosecuted and received probation, the experience caused much suffering and loss of work and money for the family. When Jared's father died of a sudden heart attack later that year, he was grief-stricken and felt responsible. He became very depressed.

The next year, Jared tried all kinds of drugs — cocaine, pills and heroin. When his mother, Jennifer Daley, confronted him, he first denied it, but then broke down and cried and asked for help to fight his addiction. Though it was a tremendous ordeal getting him into a rehab facility, they found one they felt would help. He made it through one weekend there before his insurance company forced him to move to a different facility he did not want. Jared tried to make it work, but found that it did not address the issues he was dealing with. He persevered, got out and moved away.

In 1997, following moves to Arizona and Oregon, Jared returned to Texas for a "fresh start." He got a job he liked and was planning on continuing college. Everyone was optimistic about his future. But on the morning of October 24, his mom received a phone call to call the Austin police department.

They told her that seven young people had taken heroin the night before and Jared had also taken Valium. His friends had driven him around for three hours in his own vehicle afraid to take him to the hospital. They feared that if they took him in, they would all get into trouble. Though prompt medical attention could have saved Jared's life, he was killed by fear, ignorance and a lack of societal commitment to treating those in need.

Peter McWilliams

Died in year 2000 at age 50

Died due to medical complications after being stripped of his state-endowed right to medical marijuana by a federal judge

Peter McWilliams was a king among self-help authors. Having repeatedly pulled his life together after hardships and bouts with depression, he wrote numerous books to help others rise above adversity, along with *Ain't Nobody's Business If You Do*.

Peter went through a new crisis when he was diagnosed with AIDS and cancer. Using the state-of-the-art chemotherapy "drug cocktails," he found that the cure was almost worse than the disease. Nauseous, unable to eat and bereft of appetite, Peter began to waste away at his scenic hilltop home overlooking Los Angeles. Fortunately, he found that using cannabis enabled him to use his prescribed medications and control their side effects.

He made a remarkable recovery and was once again his positive, vivacious, productive self. Even better, California voters passed Proposition 215, which legalized cultivation and use of medical marijuana in the state. Peter became an outspoken advocate. He hired activist Todd McCormick to write a book on cultivating medical marijuana, who began to grow a medical research garden. It was soon raided by the federal DEA.

Peter, McCormick and others were charged with conspiracy to cultivate and distribute cannabis. Since federal law does not allow medical use, Judge Smith forbade Peter from mentioning his medical need in court and ordered drug testing for cannabis as a term of release. Stripped of his legal defense and medical marijuana, McWilliams took a plea bargain for five years in prison and no medical marijuana. While awaiting sentencing, Peter's medication caused him to choke to death while vomiting, a symptom which cannabis had effectively controlled for years.

3. Liberty & Proportionality

Cruel and unusual punishments, private prisons

The Drug War has led to draconian mandatory minimum sentences (MMS) and asset forfeitures that are disproportionate to the offense. Federal mandatory minimum sentences put first-time, nonviolent drug offenders in prison without parole for five, ten, twenty years or even life. These are often longer terms than violent criminals receive for murder, rape or robbery, who are eligible for parole or release to reduce prison crowding.

Under federal mandatory minimums, the drug offender must serve 85 percent of the designated sentence. The penalties are rigid and unyielding, based strictly on the type and weight of a substance and the person's criminal record. Judges are not allowed to consider:

- The nature and circumstances of the offense
- The actual role of the offender in the offense
- The history and character of the defendant
- Their motivation to break the law
- The likelihood of the person to re-offend, or
- Alternative sentencing options.

Judge Franklin Billings said that MMS denies judges "the right to bring their conscience, experience, discretion and sense of what is just into the sentencing procedure, and it, in effect, makes a judge a computer, automatically imposing sentences without regard to what is right and just." The national Judicial Conference of the United States, the special Federal Courts Study Committee, 12 federal circuit courts and the American Bar Association have all called for the repeal of MMS.

The question of appropriate penalties is especially critical when an offense is not a crime with a victim who seeks restitution or retribution. Drug offenses tend to be a mutual act between consenting adults. A RAND Corporation study found that additional domestic law enforcement efforts cost 15 times as much as treatment to achieve the same reduction in societal costs.

These cruel or unusual punishments affect not only those charged with drug offenses, but others around them as well. The Drug War will take a family's breadwinner, throw them in prison, and seize their home, car and savings. It will put a family onto the welfare rolls, or take both parents and force the children to fend for themselves, to live with relatives or in separate foster homes. Such collateral damage is never calculated into the punishment given to the drug offender. Furthermore, additional penalties like property forfeiture, loss of housing, drivers' licenses, educational and medical benefits are often applied to drug offenders but *not* to violent criminals.

This is not only disproportionate to the offense, it makes it ever more difficult for drug offenders to turn their lives around. A recent study by researchers at Substance Abuse Mental Health Services Administration has indicated that 48 percent of the need for drug treatment, not including alcohol abuse, is unmet in the US. Yet, plenty of prison beds are made available.

UN Universal Declaration of Human Rights

Article 5

No one shall be subjected to torture or to cruel, inhuman or degrading treatment or punishment.

Article 4

No one shall be held in slavery or servitude; slavery and the slave trade shall be prohibited in all their forms.

Article 8

Everyone has the right to an effective remedy by the competent national tribunals for acts violating the fundamental rights granted him by the constitution or by law.

United States Constitution / Bill of Rights

Eighth Amendment

Excessive bail shall not be required, nor excessive fines imposed, nor cruel and unusual punishment inflicted.

While it condemns other countries for prison labor, the US itself regularly engages in similar activity. Prison labor and prisons for profit are touted as solutions to regional economic problems. The federal corporation, UNICOR, pays prisoners as little as 32¢ per hour to make products and provide services in competition with the private sector.

Companies like Corrections Corporation of America (CCA) and the Wackenhut Corporation market private prisons as investment opportunities and job creation programs: a twisted sort of public works project. That aspect, along with the concentration of African American men into the nation's prisons, reminds inmate Stanley Huff (page 44) of "the stench that slavery held for so many years."

These overlong drug sentences are out of proportion with other criminal penalties here in the US, as well as in comparison to the corresponding penalties in other industrial nations. The ultimate example of disproportionality is that US lawmakers enacted the death penalty — itself considered a human rights violation — for nonviolent drug offenses.

The Federal Death Penalty Formula

841(b)(1)(B) quantity X 600 = (Amount for mandatory 5 year sentence)	Death Penalty Net quantity
100 grams heroin	60 kilograms
500 g cocaine	300 kg
5 g crack	3 kg
10 g PCP (pure)	6 kg
100 g PCP (mixture)	60 kg
100 kg of marijuana	60,000 kg
100 marijuana plants	60,000 plants*
5 g methamphetamine (pure)	3 kg

Source: Criminal Justice Policy Foundation

* Non-psychoactive, industrial fiber hemp is typically seeded at more than 600,000 plants per acre. Federal law makes no distinction between hemp and marijuana.

David Ciglar

served 10 years

charged with marijuana cultivation

Before his arrest in Oakland, CA, David Ciglar was injured on his job as a firefighter/paramedic while carrying a woman from a building. He is credited with saving over 100 lives and was being retrained for a promising new career: MRI technician. Based on a tip to the DEA, he was caught with a tray of 167 marijuana seedlings in his garage. David pled guilty after prosecutors threatened that his wife would also be sent to prison and their children sent to a foster home. His family home was seized, and he received a mandatory minimum sentence of ten years.

"My family is devastated," wrote David. "My wife is living every day wondering if she can make it financially and mentally. My kids don't know why their dad was taken away for such a long, long time. I have not even bonded with my youngest daughter. She was just two when I left her. It will be proven in the near future that this is a miracle plant and the federal government has destroyed my life over it."

Is the community really safer for having locked a hero like David Ciglar behind bars for a decade?

James Geddes

serving 90 years

charged with cultivation and possession of five marijuana plants. State of Oklahoma

James (right) with his brother, E.C., and his mother

In 1992, James Geddes was walking along a street with a friend when he got arrested. The police got a search warrant and went to the home his friend rented. Although he was a frequent visitor, there was no evidence that James lived there. They found a small amount of prepared marijuana, smoking paraphernalia and five cannabis plants growing in the vegetable garden.

James refused to plea bargain, proclaimed his innocence and lost. He was also charged with possession of a firearm (which was later overturned) and some paraphernalia. He was handed a state sentence of 75 years plus one day for cultivation and another 75 years plus one day for possession, for a total of more than 150 years. James was stunned. He filed an appeal on his sentence. In 1995, his appeal came through and reduced it to 90 years.

"I honestly feel like I have been kidnapped by the state of Oklahoma. I have never murdered anyone, raped anyone, or hurt any children.

"People feel they have the right to choose their sexual preference. If they want to inject nicotine into their lungs, if they want to drug themselves with alcohol, but because I choose to smoke a little marijuana, I have to go to prison for years, maybe the rest of my life.

"How can it be that the President, his wife, the Vice President and his wife, the mayor of Washington DC, even the Speaker of the House can do these things, but I must pay dearly?"

Loren Pogue

age 67, serving 22 years

charged with conspiracy to import drugs and money laundering

Loren Pogue was the unsuspecting victim of a reverse sting operation set up by a personal acquaintance.

Pogue was an upstanding member of his community; a missionary, former serviceman, Mason, Shriner, Lions Club Member, American Legion, VFW, and past director of Children's Home who has adopted 15 children. Helping a part-time employee close a land sale in Costa Rica sent this real estate agent to prison for 22 years.

The man pleaded with Loren to help him sell a plot of land on a Costa Rican mountainside to a group of "investors." In reality, they were undercover agents pretending to shop for a place to build an airstrip. Pogue never saw nor spoke with any of the agents prior to that one meeting. It turned out his employee was a government informant, paid to the tune of $250,000.

The facts that Pogue had no drug history; that the airstrip was never built; and that, even if built, it would be useless because of its location; none of this played any part in the court's decision.

Loren went "from a happy, joyful life in a two hour meeting to pain, hurt and suffering." His family cannot afford to visit him because he is being held 1500 miles away.

"There were no drugs involved. The government agents said they were going to fly 1000 kilos of drugs into the US and that is what I was sentenced on."

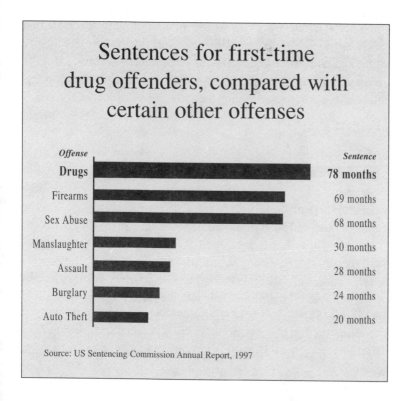

Sentences for first-time drug offenders, compared with certain other offenses

Offense	Sentence
Drugs	**78 months**
Firearms	69 months
Sex Abuse	68 months
Manslaughter	30 months
Assault	28 months
Burglary	24 months
Auto Theft	20 months

Source: US Sentencing Commission Annual Report, 1997

4. Health and Well-Being

Pain medication, needle exchange, medical marijuana

The Drug War is so intent on enforcing a "drug free America" that it routinely infringes on the appropriate use of medicine.

When are drugs appropriate? Doctors are carefully trained to make this judgement, but the decision has been co-opted by the federal Drug Enforcement Administration. The DEA, in effect, practices medicine without a license. It regulates prescriptions and sets procedures, which it may or may not follow. When determining drug classifications, federal law requires three conditions for schedule 1 (prohibited). DEA has never shown scientific cause as to why cannabis is listed there. DEA and the National Institute on Drug Abuse stifle and deny research that could rectify the problem. NIDA controls the criteria and supply of cannabis. It insists that studies be designed to show negative results. For example, Dr. Donald Abrams had to redesign his study away from researching the benefits of cannabis for AIDS patients to instead study the possibility that cannabis might interfere with other drugs. The result: it does help.

In 1999, the US Institute of Medicine confirmed the medical value of marijuana. The UN *Single Convention Treaty on Narcotic Drugs* says that "medical use of narcotic drugs (cannabis, coca, opium) continues to be indispensable for the relief of pain and suffering, and that adequate provisions must be made to ensure the[ir] availability." Voters in eight states legalized medical marijuana; yet, it remains unchanged at the federal level. Patients are still prosecuted and imprisoned for using it. In 1988, DEA administrative law judge Francis Young described that policy as "unreasonable, arbitrary and capricious."

The same cruel and autocratic attitude is seen in the federal approach to prescribed drugs, specifically, narcotics for chronic pain. When police took pain drugs away from one patient and jailed him overnight, he died from resulting trauma and shock.

Virginia physician Dr. William Hurwitz understands that adequate dosages of narcotics are needed to control pain. When he treated patients whose primary physicians would not prescribe strong enough doses, the DEA seized his license to prescribe all medications. The action stranded hundreds of patients with no source of relief. One killed himself as a result; another went for an assisted suicide. Hurwitz's case remains unresolved.

Inmates report that health care in prisons is often inadequate. Many have complained that their ailments are being ignored or neglected and procedures postponed to the point that a more serious or catastrophic condition results. In California, women inmates have died of breast cancer and other ailments that were neglected for too long. See Amnesty International Report (page 65) for more on this kind of human rights abuse.

Another health violation is the thwarting of clean needle exchange programs by prosecuting those who offer the services to people who suffer from addiction. Syringe exchanges dispense to users clean needles, condoms, and non-judgmental health information about safe sex and less harmful drug practices. Blocking them condemns many intravenous drug users, their sex partners, and offspring to preventable exposure to potentially fatal diseases. The Surgeon General reported in 2000 that "There is conclusive scientific evidence that syringe exchange programs, as part of a comprehensive HIV prevention strategy, are an effective public health intervention that reduces transmission of HIV and does not encourage the illegal use of drugs." Nonetheless, the US continues to ban funding them, and states continue to arrest community health workers.

UN Universal Declaration of Human Rights
Article 25.1
Everyone has the right to a standard of living adequate for the health and well-being of himself and of his family, including food, clothing, housing and medical care and necessary social services.

Thomas James Lowe

served 5 years

*Crohn's Disease patient
charged with marijuana cultivation,
aiding and abetting*

Thomas James (T.J.) Lowe was a San Diego photographer and naturopathic physician who used herbs and plants to treat his own Crohn's Disease and to heal others. A doctor at a VA hospital advised T.J. that cannabis with licorice root extract and ginseng might relieve his cramps, nausea and loss of appetite. He began to grow cannabis for himself and AIDS, MS and glaucoma patients, and helped patients set up three other indoor gardens.

In 1993, the gardens were discovered. Charged federally with cultivation, aiding and abetting, T.J. was sentenced to 87 months. He was promptly beaten by gang members and confined to 'the hole' — a maximum security lockdown isolation cell — for 60 days. He was transferred to Lompoc prison, where he collapsed and was taken to a hospital for emergency surgery for an intestinal obstruction. Since this was not a prison facility, he was shackled and chained to his bed for 30 days, watched over by armed guards. Due to the danger of a rupture, severe diverticula and tissue mass, the doctor recommended a second surgery to remove twelve inches of colon.

Instead, the prison transferred him to Fort Worth, where doctors gave him heavy doses of drugs that caused liver damage, then took them away. He refused to take other medication to prevent further damage. In prison, T.J. acquired cannabis to relieve his symptoms. In 1997, he failed a drug test and was sent to the hole for 30 days. In 1998, he was sentenced to nine months in the hole for the same reason.

When T.J. was released in 1999, he still had five years of supervised release. If a drug test suggests marijuana, he will be sent back to prison. While in prison, T.J. lost his wife and possessions. He didn't see his children for over five years.

James Cox

sentenced to 15 years; served 5, now on 10 years parole;

cancer, radiation poisoning patient charged with marijuana cultivation

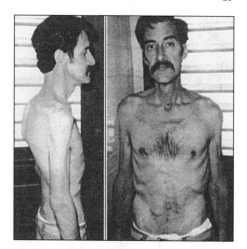

James Cox discovered medical marijuana after two surgeries for testicular cancer that metastasized to his stomach. It helped ease his pain, nausea and eating disorders caused by cancer, chemotherapy and radiation therapy. Marijuana also helped his appetite.

James was prescribed the narcotic Demerol, for 15 years and became addicted. Cannabis enabled him to get off the debilitating drug and regain control of his life. James could not afford prices on the illegal market, so he grew his own. While investigating a burglary at his home, police discovered his garden.

James and his wife, Pat, were arrested and the St. Louis, MO, home they had inherited from her mother was confiscated. James was sentenced to 15 years and Pat to five. Emotionally devastated, they attempted suicide but were revived. Their sentences were given a stay and they went home. A free man, James' desire to live returned, and he went back to growing his medicine. His health improved, but two years later, he was arrested again for his garden. This time they locked him away.

Without adequate health care in prison, he was near death. It took two stomach surgeries to save him. "Since I have been incarcerated and deprived of cannabis, I have lived in constant discomfort. My stomach deteriorated to where I could not eat anything due to incurable bleeding ulcers," James wrote.

After almost five years in prison, James went home. But he will be on parole for ten years, and drug tested twice a week for three. Doctors prescribe morphine for him. As a result, he tested positive for opiates, and they threatened to send him back to prison for legally medicating his pain to a tolerable threshold.

"I paid my debt to society; at least that's what I thought until I realized that I was still in a prison — just one without bars. Labeled a convicted drug felon; piss tests, piss tests and more piss tests; invading every aspect of my life; monthly questionnaires; surprise home visits. Freedom? Will I ever be free of pain and feel the relief that only marijuana can give me? No more ugly green bars. I am thankful for that, but will I ever be truly free? Will I ever be done with my debt to society?"

Will Foster

sentenced to 93 years, reduced to 20

rheumatoid arthritis patient charged with marijuana cultivation

William Foster was a productive citizen who paid taxes, served in the Army, and had his own computer programmer/analyst business for five years. He, his wife Megan, and their three children were leading ordinary lives in Oklahoma until he was arrested for his choice of medicine.

Will has crippling rheumatoid arthritis in his feet, hips, lower back and hands. He did not like the side effects of the drugs his doctors prescribed. The highly addictive drugs left him moody, tired and edgy, making it difficult for him to enjoy his family or do his job. Will found that marijuana controlled his pain and swelling without the side effects.

Just after Christmas in 1995, police entered the Fosters' home with a 'John Doe' search warrant for methamphetamine, citing a 'confidential informant.' They found no evidence of anything listed on the search warrant, but they did find his basement garden of 66 cannabis plants — and $28 cash.

Will refused a 'deal' and asked for a jury trial. At trial, Foster was not allowed to present a medical defense, nor was he able to confront the witnesses against him, despite the Sixth Amendment. The jury convicted him. Will was sentenced to 93 years — 70 for cultivation, 20 for possession in the presence of a minor (his own child), two for intent to distribute, and one for not having a tax stamp.

Since his incarceration, Will has had insufficient medical treatment. He risks losing his left leg from the knee down, due to swelling that is inadequately treated. In 1998, a parole board ruled that his sentence "offends the conscience" and reduced it to 20 years. The board unanimously recommended Will be released, but Governor Keating rejected their recommendation.

"We were a happy, typical family that had a life and had dreams, but the Tulsa Police Department had different ideas," Will wrote. Another family shattered by drug policy.

Therapeutic Uses of Cannabis / Marijuana

Cannabis has been indicated as a medicine to help treat AIDS wasting syndrome, appetite loss, arthritis, cancer chemotherapy and radiation therapy side effects, chronic pain, cramps and muscle spasms, depression, epilepsy and convulsive disorders, glaucoma, insomnia, migraine headache, multiple sclerosis and spasticity disorders, nausea, PTSD, rheumatism, spinal cord injury, stress-related problems, vomiting and many other health symptoms and conditions.

Science has accepted Medical Marijuana

The US government spend $1 million in 1998 to have the National Academy of Science look into the medical record and studies on cannabis. The answer: Marijuana *does* have medicinal value.

Voters have accepted Medical Marijuana

States that have legalized medical marijuana and cultivation by voter initiative include Alaska, Arizona, California, Colorado, Maine, Nevada, Oregon and Washington. States that have done it by legislative action include Hawaii. More than 37 state legislatures have indicated their support for medical marijuana.

5. Personal Privacy

Invasive technology, police powers, citizen spies

Americans endure increasing invasions of privacy: phone taps, urine tests, trash, mail and email searches, computer searches of bank records and utility bills. Infrared scans of homes measure the heat they radiate. Warrantless searches are served with battering rams and guns. When warrants are issued, they are often based on surveillance, high-tech spying, or hearsay of a confidential informant; perhaps a "friend" secretly working for the police.

Police wiretapped 2.27 million conversations in 1997. They sweep neighborhoods and have used roadblocks to search people arbitrarily, sometimes using dogs. People who match a "profile" (a racial or culturally-based stereotype appearance, such as ethnicity, long hair, political or music bumper stickers, etc.) are targeted for harassment in traffic stops and on the streets. Police and schools randomly search student lockers and pay students to turn in others. Ads and billboards solicit and reward anonymous neighborhood spies. Parole and probation terms typically require the total surrender of Constitutional, privacy and medical rights.

Having $100 cash is all it takes for police to seize it as 'suspected drug income' — even when you can prove otherwise. Buying garden supplies can lead to a search of your home. Paying cash for a plane ticket or using large-denomination currency can be used against you in court.

Drug tests do not show impairment, nor have they ever been scientifically proven "safe and effective." Yet, employees are given invasive and costly drug tests without probable cause as a job requirement. Long-time employees are fired and denied pensions over test results that do not show impairment but do suggest marijuana has been consumed within the last month. This is job discrimination. Many lives are harmed by adulterated tests and "false positives" that incorrectly indicate drug metabolites. These tests even decide who has their probation or parole revoked. Parolee Mark Misenhimer was sent back to prison for a year after accidentally eating poppy-seed bread, which suggests heroin in tests.

High school students can be expelled for cannabis, and are often subjected to drug tests to participate in many school activities. They can be banned for failing a test or for refusing to take one. College students who violate any drug law lose loans and educational grants, and can be kicked out of school. Whole families are punished and can lose public housing when a single family member is accused of drug activities — even if it occurs off the premises.

The concept of Americans having a "reasonable expectation of privacy" has been turned on its head by courts that say we no longer have reason to expect privacy, due to the government's "overriding interest" in waging the Drug War. But such policy is clearly antithetical to American democracy and freedom.

UN Universal Declaration of Human Rights
Article 12
No one shall be subjected to arbitrary interference with his privacy, family, home or correspondence, nor to attacks upon his honor and reputation. Everyone has the right to the protection of the law against such interference or attacks.

United States Constitution / Bill of Rights
Fourth Amendment
The right of the people to be secure in their persons, houses, papers, and effects, against unreasonable searches and seizures, shall not be violated, and no Warrants shall issue, but upon probable cause supported by Oath or affirmation, and particularly describing the place to be searched, and the persons or things to be seized.

The Tucker Family

Gary Tucker
serving 10 years

Joanne Tucker
serving 10 years

Steve Tucker
serving 10 years

Above: Steve Tucker (left) on visiting day with his brother, Gary, and their mother, Doris.

Left: Gary's wife Joanne.

charged with conspiracy to manufacture marijuana, knowingly knowing that others were growing marijuana

In 1992, the DEA was engaged in Operation Green Merchant, a campaign to eradicate indoor marijuana cultivation across the nation. Its targets were hydroponics (indoor gardening) stores and their customers. Agents would copy down the license plate numbers of customers, follow and spy on them, steal their trash and subpoena utility bills to check for high electrical usage.

Out of Green Merchant grew Operation Triox, specifically

targeting a small garden supply store in Georgia, Southern Lights and Hydroponics, Inc. The DEA approached owner Gary Tucker, demanding to hide cameras in the shop to film customers. His refusal led to a threat to shut him down; but the Feds did much more than that before they were through with the family.

Gary, his wife Joanne, and his brother Steven Tucker were all convicted of conspiracy to manufacture marijuana, based on the offenses of a few customers with whom they had no contact other than selling them completely legal garden equipment.

The family had no marijuana on their persons, in their homes, or in the store. They were never caught growing, selling or buying cannabis, nor did they have any paraphernalia.

As Gary Tucker wrote, "My main concern is that America is becoming a police state — that we are losing our liberties and the politicians are using the drug war as an excuse."

Big Brother: Aerial police surveillance into someone's backyard in California. Photo courtesy of Humboldt County (CA) Cannabis Action Network.

Joe Pinson

served 5 years

asthma patient charged with marijuana cultivation

Joe Pinson's mother, Regina, and his grandmother, Amy, testify to all the time they spent taking care of Joe as a child due to his severe, life-threatening bouts with asthma.

Many were the times they had to rush him to the hospital as he was turning gray, unable to breathe. He missed so much school one year that he was held back a grade, and they got a private tutor to work with him at home.

Pharmaceutical drugs failed to give him relief. However, when Joe was 18, his episodes suddenly stopped. For the first time, he was able to breathe and lead a normal life. Finally, his family thought — he must have grown out of it!

Agents began investigating Joe in 1991 after he bought some growing equipment. His home utility records showed high electrical usage. The DEA, without a search warrant, scanned his Missouri property from a helicopter using a heat-sensing, infrared device. Agents got a warrant and found 150 marijuana plants in his attic. That's how his mother and grandmother found out that Joe had not outgrown his asthma, but was using cannabis as an effective medication to control it.

Prosecutors seized the family home and his mother had to pay $25,000 to get her own house back. When Pinson's lawyer protested that the fly-over constituted an unreasonable search, the judge ruled that Pinson had no reasonable expectation that the invisible heat radiating from his home was private.

Joe was handed a five year mandatory minimum sentence for growing his medicine. In prison, they did not give him his medicine of choice. Instead, they prescribed him hard drugs, such as steroids, with known harmful side effects.

6. Family

Destruction of families, effects on children and parental rights, lack of sentencing options

Though Drug War proponents claim to be "protecting kids," it is the children who have become the unseen casualties.

The family is a primary target of the Drug War, and children are often left to endure the painful, traumatic separation from their parents when long prison terms are imposed. They are sentenced to years without their parents' love, nurturing and support. How can a parent support their family, financially or emotionally, from behind prison walls?

Children are often displaced from schools and communities when their families are shattered and split apart. They may be left in a single parent home, or without a home, car or money after their parents' assets have been confiscated. Others are forced to live with extended families members or friends. When these are not options, they must fend for themselves or become wards of the state in foster homes. It is difficult to cope with the loss and anger that may result in behavioral problems or failure in school.

Meanwhile, some inmates have reported that they have lost track of their children and the ability to assert parental rights after their children entered the foster care system.

Families in urban minority communities are devastated by the Drug War, with whole generations' lives lost behind bars. Statistics show that children of prisoners are more likely to be incarcerated, as well. How can a community survive with a third of its young-adult male population bearing a criminal record, as is the case with African American neighborhoods?

Children are often home during a police raid. How does it affect them to see their parents handcuffed, face down on the floor while angry, armed men in dark suits and badges curse at them and tear the house apart? What happens to children when

police hold them at gunpoint for hours? Psychologists say that
the loss of a child's parents to prison is the emotional equivalent
of losing them to death. What crime did the little ones commit
that they should be punished so?

Sentencing options other than prison are needed for non-
violent offenders who are no threat to society. Shorter sentences,
home confinement, treatment, community service, parenting
classes, residential settings that keep mothers with their children,
and probation are just a few ways to help protect rather than
destroy the integrity of the family.

Women who use illicit drugs during pregnancy have been
drug tested in the delivery room and threatened with criminal
prosecution, and have had their infants taken
away. In divorce custody battles, parents
who drink alcohol are given preference over
an equally good parent who uses cannabis.

**Victor Plescia's daughter, Maggie, sent him this note
after he was sentenced to 35 years for a conspiracy.**

Martin Sax

serving 21.8 years

*charged with conspiracy to
distribute marijuana,
money laundering*

"My wife has been left to raise
our son all by herself. She has no
help and Benjamin has no father
to put him to bed at night. My
little boy will never know what
it's like to have his Daddy tuck him in bed, give him a kiss, and
read him a bedtime story. ... If the laws don't change, my little
boy will be 20 years old before I get out."

Kevin Alexander

serving 20 years

charged with possession with intent to distribute crack cocaine

Kevin with his family

UN Universal Declaration of Human Rights
Article 16.3
The family is the natural and fundamental group unit of society and is entitled to protection by society and the state.

Laichem Sae Lee

serving 10 years

charged with conspiracy to import and distribute opium

"I am thousands of miles away from my children. ... I have seen my children once in four years. ...

"They are not doing well with the loss of both their parents."

Because Laichem is not an American citizen, the federal government plans to deport her upon her release — taking her even farther away from her own children.

Lovetta Clark

serving 30 years

charged with conspiracy to import and distribute cocaine

"My children are the ones that are suffering the most. My son, Stanley, always asked me, 'Mama, when are you coming home?' I replied, 'Soon.' After six years he said, 'Mama, soon sure takes a long, long time.' "

**A Drug War POW's son sent
her this hand-made card.**

Crystal, right, wearing glasses

*How it
happened*
By Crystal Nelson

My mom used to tuck her four kids in bed at
night, and one night after she had tucked us
all in, the police came jumping through our
windows, breaking down doors, and worst of all,
pointing guns at everyone in the house. …

The day that my parents and brothers were
taken to prison, I felt like my heart had
jumped out of my chest and onto the ground, I
hurt so bad. … When I was 15 years old, I had
a summer job. I sent my parents money to help
with their personal needs while in prison. My
Mom makes 12¢ per hour, and my Dad $50 a month.
Whenever I scrape up enough money to send to
them, I do it. …

I take my 6-year-old cousin, 3-year-old
cousin, and 6-month-old nephew to church,
because I feel they should know about God
before their life starts getting harder. I
learned the hard way, but I still thank God for
keeping my family in contact.

7. Racism and Discrimination

Targeting inner city and minority communities

The US prison population includes a disproportionately high number of minorities. About 51 percent of state and federal inmates are African American and 15 percent Hispanic. The majority are serving time for non-violent property and drug crimes.

Almost one in three African American males in their twenties are under some form of criminal justice supervision — either in prison, on probation or on parole. This has resulted in the disenfranchisement of a large segment of the community. It contributes to the break up families and erosion of participation in the community, along with the removal of voting rights.

Mandatory minimums are discriminatory in application, creating racially-based sentencing disparities. Despite being almost identical pharmaceutical compounds, it takes five grams of crack cocaine or 500 grams of powder cocaine to trigger a five year federal mandatory minimum sentence: a hundred-fold disparity. White Americans admit higher rates of crack use than Blacks, but African Americans are serving 88 percent of the prison sentences for crack — sentences that average 28 percent longer than whites convicted of the same activity. Congress has continually failed to rectify this disparity.

Law enforcement has admitted to racial profiling in traffic stops and often targets inner city neighborhoods where street activity is more visible. "Neighborhood sweeps" of economically depressed areas round up desperate people who are lured into the drug trade by the opportunity for quick cash. A lack of educational opportunities and jobs in poverty-stricken areas opens up a virtual "revolving door" to prison. Rather than solve the underlying root causes of this social problem, the US instead has chosen to invest in incarceration.

Congressmember Maxine Waters held hearings in 1998 that not only corroborate this disparity, but also developed evidence that the CIA actually may have been involved in targeting inner city communities for cocaine smuggled in by US military allies in Central America to finance unauthorized foreign wars.

This begs the question: Did African Americans win freedom from slavery only to become slaves of the prison industry?

UN Universal Declaration of Human Rights
Article 2
Everyone is entitled to all the rights and freedoms set forth in this Declaration, without distinction of any kind, such as race, color, sex, language, religion, political or other opinion, national or social origin, property, birth or other status.

Furthermore, no distinction shall be made on the basis of the political, jurisdictional or international status of the country or territory to which a person belongs, whether it be independent, trust, non-self-governing or under any other limitation of sovereignty.
Article 7
All are equal before the law and are entitled without any discrimination to equal protection of the law. All are entitled to equal protection against any discrimination in violation of this Declaration and against any incitement to such discrimination.

United States Constitution / Bill of Rights
Fourteenth Amendment
All persons born or naturalized in the United States and subject to the jurisdiction thereof, are citizens of the United States and of the State wherein they reside.

No State shall make or enforce any law which shall abridge the privileges or immunities of citizens of the United States ... nor deny to any person within its jurisdiction the equal protection of the laws.

Everett Gholston, III

serving 12 years, 7 months

charged with conspiracy to distribute cocaine

"If the government keeps up this pace, the Black male and family will become extinct."

"Shomari"
Stanley Huff

serving 15 years

charged with trafficking a half-kilo of cocaine

"A friend and I made a list of all the men and women that have been charged or sentenced under federal drug laws for crack. We came up with 48 names, all Black ... not one white. Creating 'selective prosecution' laws ... reeks the stench that slavery held for so many years."

Michael Clarke

serving 13 years

*charged with possession
of crack cocaine with
intent to distribute*

**Michael, center, seen with
his mother and family
members.**

Michael Clarke was a senior at North Carolina Central University, majoring in visual communication and art.

He was engaged to a young woman who was a student at the UNC, Chapel Hill campus.

They had great plans. Unfortunately, his mother got injured, which led the family to serious financial trouble. Michael took part-time jobs, "but that did not even put a dent in the problem."

He was desperate and thought he had found a way out. He began to sell crack. As his economic woes began to subside, new problems arose. His schoolwork and relationship began to suffer. At his fiancee's urging, he quit dealing. She was pregnant, and they were close to graduating and reaching their dreams.

When Michael got robbed, his money problems arose again. "The answer came wrapped in a beautifully packaged box with ignorance hiding inside with a one-way ticket to destruction," he wrote. Like a Trojan Horse, this apparent gift ultimately turned out to be holding the seeds of Michael's destruction. He was arrested after two individuals set him up to take the fall for them.

"I made a mistake, but my sentence is drastically exaggerated. My mistake is being used to stuff ballot boxes. It doesn't take 13 years to realize that there are legal ways to empower yourself financially. ...

"This is not rehabilitation, this is production of hardened criminals, destruction of families. Suppression of the effects will not solve the problem until the real causes are addressed.

"I'm the effect, not the cause. I say 'Justice'."

8. Private Property

Due process, property rights, conflicts of interest

Civil asset forfeiture laws allow the government to seize personal, private property without charging anyone with a crime, and then keep it with only a minimal link to criminal misconduct — and not necessarily that of the owner. Since regaining property requires a large financial bond plus high legal costs, often upward of $15,000, few people fight seizures of less than $20,000 value.

In forfeiture law, it is the property that is accused of a crime, not the owner. Unlike people, property does not have any legal rights, so self-serving prosecutors are unbridled to run wild. They are limited only to "probable cause," a vague standard equivalent to nothing more than suspicion. Even property of innocent owners has been seized and kept (Bennis v. Michigan).

> "Civil asset forfeiture laws are being used in terribly unjust ways, depriving innocent citizens of their property with nothing that can be called due process. ... You never have to be convicted of any crime to lose your property. You never have to be charged with any crime. In fact, even if you are acquitted by a jury on criminal charges, your property can be seized."
> — *U.S. Rep. Henry Hyde (R, IL)*

> "A law designed to give cops the right to confiscate and keep the luxury possessions of major drug dealers mostly ensnares the modest homes, cars and hard-earned cash of ordinary law-abiding people. This was not the way it was supposed to work."
> — *U.S. Rep. John Conyers (D, MI)*

Seized property — homes, cars, or life savings — is presumed guilty and may be forfeited based upon hearsay, or even a tip supplied by an informant who stands to financially benefit from the proceedings by collecting a percentage. Police and secret informants can divide up and keep the assets they confiscate, creating an obvious conflict of interest. A procedural hearing is held to determine the outcome, thus circumventing the right to a jury trial, as stipulated in the Seventh Amendment, thus circumventing the US Constitution.

The abuses became so rampant that Congress finally modified the federal law to eliminate the bond and require a conviction. However, state laws still vary widely, and the Drug War model has since spawned myriad forfeiture laws for taking people's property in response to a whole range of offenses, from soliciting drugs or a prostitute to zoning violations.

The Drug War has laid the groundwork for the US to become a literal "kleptocracy:" government by theft.

UN Universal Declaration of Human Rights
Article 17.2
No one shall be arbitrarily deprived of his property.

United States Constitution / Bill of Rights
Fifth Amendment
No person shall be … deprived of life, liberty, or property, without due process of law; nor shall private property be taken for public use, without just compensation.

Seventh Amendment
In Suits at common law, where the value in controversy shall exceed \$20, the right of trial by jury shall be preserved, and no fact tried by a jury shall be otherwise re-examined in any Court of the United States, than according to the rules of the common law.

Scott Walt

serving 24¹/₂ years

charged with conspiracy to possess marijuana with intent to distribute

"[The agent] said to me, 'We want to search your house. If we have to get a warrant we will bust your doors down, put guns to your wife and children's heads and tear your f-ing house apart, or you can sign this waiver and we'll be nice.' Well, I signed the waiver. ... They found no drugs, no scales, no ledgers, nothing!

"My wife was a team leader for Mary Kay Cosmetics and her office was in our home. They took financial records, a cell phone, our home phone, address book, and $7,350 in our bedroom. She asked, 'Why are you taking the money.' They said, 'drug proceeds.' We shook our heads in disbelief. ...

"At sentencing the government wanted a fine of $250,000. ... The judge said, 'No fine. This man is getting far too much time; murderers receive less. If it weren't for the book, (he held up the sentencing guidelines), I would not be sentencing him to this. Enough is enough!'"

Alfreda Robinson

serving 10 years

charged with conspiracy to distribute crack cocaine

Alfreda Robinson worked as a high school counselor in Baltimore, MD. When her son David was arrested, he naturally called his mom from jail and asked her to help.

He needed money for an attorney, and a friend owed him some. He asked Alfreda to phone his friend's mother to get $4500 from them to help cover his legal expenses. By placing this call, she became vulnerable as a 'conspirator' in his case.

Her son was released and came home. The morning of the raid, the $4500 in marked bills was found in her basement safe, placed there by David without her knowledge. Despite a complete lack of evidence placing Alfreda near any drug activity, the government used this money to seize her house, which had been legally purchased with documented and verified funds from an automobile settlement.

Her son's "friend" turned informant and got immunity for his testimony that resulted in a 45-year sentence for David and ten years for Alfreda. Prison was the price of her motherly love.

The Kubinski Family

Kenny Kubinski
serving natural life

Jackie Kubinski
sentenced to 6-1/2 years, served 5+

charged with conspiracy to distribute cocaine, hashish and marijuana

In separate prison visits, Jackie Kubinski and her husband, Kenny, are surrounded by their children, Adam, Ariel and Katie.

Before their arrest, the Kubinskis were active members of their farm community.

Kenny cut and delivered firewood to elderly neighbors, volunteered his landscaping skills to Habitat for Humanity through the church, and provided jobs through his family construction company. Jackie was an active member at her church, a volunteer at her children's school, and a local board member for the American Diabetes Association.

Due to asset forfeiture, the family lost everything: their home, business, freedom and, for years, each other. Following a traumatic separation, the children are learning to cope. Jackie wrote, "They always ask, 'When are you coming home?'" Before her release, the children were able to visit Jackie once a month for a few hours at a time. They can only visit their father every three or four months, because the prison is so far away.

Adam drew this picture and asked, "Mommy, is there a hole where my house was?"

Open letter from Jackie Kubinski

"On January 15, 1993, a Government Drug Task Force came to our house at seven a.m. and said the government was seizing all our property, personal and corporate. No drugs were found and no arrests were made at the time the property was seized. The government alleged that my husband acquired his business with drug proceeds and used the business to launder money....

"On April 30, 1993, we were arrested. The government did everything they could to prevent us from hiring a lawyer. When the company made money to pay bills, it would be seized by the IRS from the corporation account. We are presently destitute.

"I was charged with misprision of a felony* [later dropped] and money laundering. Then a few months later they added a superseding indictment charge, dropped the money laundering charge and added conspiracy to distribute cocaine, hashish and marijuana. I began serving my sentence in November, 1994.

"Our children were put in an orphanage until friends from our church asked for custody. I am presently in a prison for women in Butner, North Carolina.

"Our son Adam would get so mad, because he couldn't do anything to help get his mom and dad out of jail. On Thanksgiving day, he cried, 'I just want my own mom and dad and my own turkey and my own table.'"

---

* Withholding knowledge of a felony by someone who was not involved in it.

9. Freedom of Religion & Culture

Religious persecution, cultural and lifestyle suppression, community infiltration, drug-culture profiles

Despite the First Amendment, Congress and the DEA have suppressed the practice of all traditional religions that use cannabis as a sacrament, such as the Rastafari, Coptic Christians, Sufi Moslem and Sadhu Hindu. The government forbids every effort to establish new religions that involve the use of mind-expanding drugs, and only government-approved sacraments are allowed, blurring the line between church and state.

When the Drug War even infringed on the Native American Church's ceremonial use of peyote, Congress passed a special exemption, the Religious Freedom Restoration Act. The Supreme Court struck it down, and courts routinely exclude all testimony or reference to any religious use when "the facts" of a case are

Below: a group of Deadheads posed together in a federal prison in NY, 1995.

presented to a jury. This is done on both a state and federal level, stripping religious protections of any practical value.

The Drug War targets subcultures identified as part of 'the drug culture'. Hippies and fans of music like jazz, reggae, hip-hop, house, psychedelic, and the Grateful Dead are singled out for persecution. Police periodically barricade roads leading to political rallies and cultural events, and they search, harass and intimidate attendees. Dance culture and rave events are targeted. Freedom in America apparently no longer includes the right to express yourself, have fun or engage in the "Pursuit of Happiness" — unless the corporate alcohol and tobacco lobbies sponsor or profit from your choice of lifestyle.

UN Universal Declaration of Human Rights
Article 18
Everyone has the right to freedom of thought, conscience and religion: This right includes freedom to change his religion or belief, and freedom, either alone or in community with others and in public or private, to manifest his religion or belief in teaching, practice, worship and observance.

Article 27.1
Everyone has the right freely to participate in the cultural life of the community, to enjoy the arts and to share in scientific advancement and its benefits.

United States Constitution / Bill of Rights
First Amendment
Congress shall make no law respecting an establishment of religion, or prohibiting the free exercise thereof; or abridging the freedom of speech, or of the press; or the right of the people peaceably to assemble, and to petition the Government for a redress of grievances.

Calvin Treiber
serving 29 years

Jodie Israel
sentenced to 11 years, served 7

charged with marijuana conspiracy. Jodie received presidential clemency in 2001.

Jodie and Calvin with one of their daughters.

Jodie Israel was indicted for a marijuana conspiracy involving her Rastafarian husband, Calvin Treiber, and 24 others in Montana. The FBI dubbed it 'Operation Reggae North,' since most of the defendants were Rastafarians — a distinctive cultural group that believes that 'ganja' and its smoke are forms of a religious sacrament that brings them closer to God.

Jodie was charged with possession of less than two ounces of cannabis, an alleged sale of four ounces (with no evidence), money laundering, and conspiracy. Both are first-time, non-violent offenders. They believe their case is an example of religious persecution, political harassment and selective prosecution.

Their long sentences have been particularly difficult for their four children, who've been virtually 'orphaned' by the government, and separated from each other to live in different homes.

"Adults should realize that marijuana should not be even put in the same category as hard drugs. Herb is a naturally-grown plant that has not been processed by man into some incredibly potent chemical drug. It is far less harmful for people than alcohol or cigarettes. So why take people's lives and put them in prison forever for it?" asks Calvin.

Open letter from Jodie Israel

"After many hours of sitting in a holding tank [waiting to be transferred to another prison], we were told we would be sleeping on the floor of the holding tank with a mattress.

"One woman had had a baby two weeks prior by Cesarean section, and it would have been very difficult for her. We were finally given a room, a vinyl mattress, and a wool blanket — no sheet or pillow, or sleeping clothes.

"From the window in our cell block, I watched a man in a steel, closed-in cell, with a food tray opening in the door, and a very small four by six inch window. What I saw I will never forget. The jail had a phone on wheels, they rolled up to the food tray slot. As I watched him dialing and then hanging up before there was even time for a connection, I assumed he was just dialing for something to do. It was awful to see a human being caged like an animal.

"An older woman with us told me that her husband was very ill, and they had left a halfway house, so they could spend what might have been their last days together. While we were in the holding tank, the men were marched by in groups to be processed. As I watched, an older man in the group walked by with a cane. His wife spotted him and they looked at each other and held their hands up at each other. It was heartbreaking to think that will probably be her last memory of him.

"After the men were processed, we were taken out of the holding cell, five at a time to be strip searched, and then shackled and chained. After all the women were ready, we were taken to a long corridor, about 1/2 mile long. Along the right hand side of the corridor was prisoner after prisoner, all shackled and chained. Instead of feeling human, it felt more like we were cattle being shipped to the slaughter house, so dehumanizing.

"The sight of so many prisoners and of how their families will suffer and what they will have to endure made me ill. It was a sight I will never be able to get out of my mind."

Rev. Tom Brown

sentenced to 5 years

Founder and pastor of 'Our Church', which uses sacramental cannabis in its religious services, charged with marijuana cultivation

Founded in 1988 and incorporated in 1994, "Our Church" is recognized by the state of Arkansas as a tax-exempt religion, and uses the cannabis flower and peyote among its sacraments.

Reverend Tom Brown, a licensed minister of Our Church, follows its creed to use God-given herbs and plants for spiritual insight. He was determined to exercise his religious rights. He deeded one acre of his 39-acre blueberry farm to the church for its members to grow their holy plants. Along with ten other church members, he met with the local county sheriff to explain the plan and promised not to sell any. They cited the Religious Freedom Restoration Act (later over-turned by the Supreme Court) and asserted their basic human right to grow plants and share their sacrament under freedom of religion.

In August, 1994, Rev. Brown was arrested and charged with the manufacture of 435 marijuana plants and three peyote plants. During his trial, he was not allowed to present a religious defense or even to mention Our Church.

Brown was sentenced to ten years in prison (later reduced to five, due to a change in federal plant-weight calculations). His entire farm was seized, even though his "crime" of practicing religious freedom was not committed there, but on a separately deeded parcel of land belonging to the church.

10. Livelihood, Tolerance & Equal Rights

Industrial hemp, zero tolerance, bigotry, discrimination

The lies and brutality of the Drug War have created a nation of second-class citizens stripped of their most basic rights.

The Drug War harms economic opportunity, jobs and free enterprise by banning domestic production of industrial hemp. This non-drug, seed and fiber variety of cannabis is so valuable that other nations subsidize it. Presidents Washington and Jefferson, both hemp farmers, would face the death penalty for growing this plant the government now mislabels as "marijuana." Several states have passed bills to restore hemp farming, but the federal government blocks interstate commerce and intrastate production of this crop, violating people's economic human right to engage in traditional means of livelihood.

The level of marijuana arrests shows bias against a sizable population. Some 71 million Americans have tried it. In 1999 704,812 people were arrested for cannabis, 88 percent for possession only. Meanwhile, alcohol and tobacco are promoted.

The federal policy of "zero tolerance" is achieved by stigmatizing and criminalizing cultures, individuals and lifestyles. Being arrested at college over drugs can lead to expulsion, loss of financial aid, and other serious damage to one's lifetime earning potential. Being labeled a drug felon makes it difficult to find gainful employment. Even in grammar school, any infraction of "zero tolerance" can easily stain a student's permanent record, follow them for life and strip them of job opportunities. Incidents that have triggered this include sharing aspirin, throat lozenges, an asthma inhaler during an attack, giving a teacher wine for a gift; even wearing a plastic sword on Halloween.

What message are we sending to children? DARE (Drug

A DARE officer plays with a student in Oakland, CA

Abuse Resistance Education) puts police into grammar schools to talk to children about the private lives of their parents and friends. Studies by the American Psychological Association and others find that the program has no long-term effect on adolescent drug use, and may actually lead to increased drug use in some groups. Personal betrayal is rewarded. DARE students have been encouraged to turn in their parents for drugs, which has led to arrests and breakup of families. When Leo Mercado decided to keep his child out of DARE, his Kearney, AZ family became the subject of a police investigation.

Intolerance breeds bigotry and human rights abuses. It is the Drug War that should not be tolerated. The rights of all people must be restored and respected. It is clearly the duty of "We the People" to restore liberty and justice for all.

UN Universal Declaration of Human Rights
Article 23.1
Everyone has the right to work, to free choice of employment, to just and favorable conditions of work and to protection against unemployment

Article 26.2
Education shall be directed to the full development of the human personality and to the strengthening of respect for humans rights and fundamental freedoms. It shall promote understanding, tolerance and friendship. …

Article 26.3
Parents have a prior right to choose the kind of education that shall be given to their children.

11. Conclusion: A Ray of Hope

Persevere. After serving nine years of her 24-year prison sentence, and during the final months of President Bill Clinton's term of office, Amy Ralston Pofahl (page 8) received a Presidential Clemency. She was one of about two dozen nonviolent drug offenders clemencies from among the estimated 400,000 such people incarcerated in the US. Six of these inmates were featured in the Human Rights and the Drug War project.

Events since 1996 show that the public opinion tide has turned on the cost and benefits of the Drug War. That has not, however, kept the US from expanding into armed conflict in Colombia or escalating the war within its own borders.

Beginning with California's Proposition 215 and sweeping across the nation, voters have endorsed medical marijuana and created legal protection for patients to use it. A growing national movement for Drug War amnesty has taken form, with clergy in its forefront and compassion as its theme. California voters passed Prop 36 in 2000, firmly putting voters on the side of treatment rather than incarceration for drug offenders. Now we

The authors gathered with Amy Ralston Pofahl to celebrate her July 7, 2000, release on a Presidential Clemency from Bill Clinton. Left to right: Virginia Resner, Amy, Mikki Norris and Chris Conrad

have a new administration, but laws and entrenched policies still need to be changed. That is the bottom line. This is an opportunity to see if regulation can succeed where prohibition has failed.

Elected officials need to hear from their constituents, over and over again. There are national vigils, teach-ins, voter initiatives and lobbying campaigns. If this book touches your heart or conscience, you have a role to play. We urge you to become part of the solution. Please network with and support Human Rights and the Drug War and other organizations listed on page 68 of this book. You can make a difference.

Join us in urging all Americans, the UN and the world community to hold US drug policy accountable to human rights law.

Kemba Smith

served 10 years of a 24 year sentence

charged with a cocaine conspiracy attributed to an abusive boyfriend in which she was only minimally involved

Presidential clemency, 2000

Antoinette Frink

served 8 of a 15-¹/₂ year sentence

owner of a car dealership who was charged with cocaine conspiracy for the activities of individuals who were arrested in vehicles they had bought or retitled from her company.

Presidential clemency, 2001

Antoinette (r) and a friend with her daughter Trina, kneeling, who died in a car accident driving home from visiting her mom in prison.

Appendix: The Human Rights and the Drug War Project

Human Rights and the Drug War exhibit at San Francisco Main Library, 1998.

This book is based on the Human Rights and the Drug War photo and information exhibit, originally known as HR 95.

This museum-quality exhibit began in 1995 in San Francisco, in conjunction with the UN's 50th anniversary activities, as an opportunity to bring awareness to the world community and general public about the human casualties and costs of the Drug War. It was initiated by the Family Council on Drug Awareness and California Families Against Mandatory Minimums (FAMM). Since its inception, it has been shown at community centers, libraries, churches, universities, public buildings, conferences, and festivals throughout the US and Europe.

To meet the growing demand for this popular exhibit, we have turned to creating lightweight, weatherproof laminated versions of this educational display for sale or rent to groups and organizations. There are currently 30 sets in distribution. The material is also available at our website, www.hr95.org, and as a slide presentation.

In 1998, we released the first edition of our book, *Shattered Lives: Portraits from America's Drug War*. It expands on the exhibit materials and topics, and gives a face and voice to a large number of prisoners of the Drug War — America's new POWs — who are locked away out of sight, but nonetheless need to be seen and heard.

This project is a work in progress. We continue to collect case histories, photos, and research related to the Drug War and develop other media to disseminate this important material, because, unfortunately, the need to expose these human rights violations goes on.

We have no corporate sponsors or paid staff. This exhibit is supported through the donations and voluntary activity of people like you. Fiscal sponsorship can be arranged for tax-exempt donations. Your support will help us to further explore and expose the human rights violations of the US Drug War

Thanks for your consideration and for whatever action you take.

To help, or for more info on the exhibit project or our books, please contact:

Human Rights and the Drug War

HRDW
PO Box 1716,
El Cerrito CA
94530 USA.

Phone/fax:
510-215-8326

Email:
Mikki@hr95.org
Website:
www.hr95.org

What Are Human Rights?

Among the rights for each person which the United Nations encoded into the Universal Declaration of Human Rights are:

- Article 1: All human beings are born free and equal in dignity and rights. They are endowed with reason and conscience and should act toward one another in a spirit of brotherhood.
- Art. 2: Freedom from discrimination.
- Art. 3: Life, liberty and security of person
- Art. 4: Freedom from slavery in any form
- Art. 5: Freedom from torture and cruel, inhuman or degrading treatment or punishment
- Art.6: Right to recognition as a person before the law
- Art. 7: Equal protection from discrimination and violations of Human Rights and from incitement to such treatment
- Art. 8: Right to remedy by competent tribunal
- Art. 10: Right to a fair and impartial public hearing of all legal charges
- Art. 11: Right to be considered innocent until proven guilty.
- Art. 12, Art. 16: Security of privacy, family, home or correspondence, and from attacks against your honor and reputation
- Art. 17: Right to property
- Art. 18: Freedom of religion, belief and religious practice
- Art. 19: Freedom of opinion and information
- Art. 20: Freedom of peaceful assembly and association
- Art 21: Right to participate in government and in free elections
- Art. 22: Cultural rights and personal dignity
- Art. 23: Free choice of employment and protection against unemployment; just and favorable remuneration for labor
- Art. 25: Right to health and well-being, food, clothing, housing, medical care and necessary social services, and security in event of loss of livelihood
- Art. 26: Right to education promoting understanding and tolerance
- Art. 27: Right freely to participate in the cultural life of the community, to enjoy the arts, and to share in scientific advancement and benefits
- Art. 29: Rights and freedoms only subject to such limitations as are required to secure the rights and freedoms of others in a just and moral public order.

Human Rights Watch Report: 2000

The US Drug War is responsible for the dramatic increase in prison population, Human Rights Watch made the direct connection in its June, 2000 report.

Human Rights Watch stated that drug policies "bear the prime responsibility for the quadrupling of the national prison population since 1980 and a soaring incarceration rate, the highest among western democracies." It reported that more people are being sent to prison for non-violent drug offenses than for violent crimes.

In analyzing the prison population, the Human Rights Watch report found disturbing racial disparities between blacks and whites in rates of arrest, conviction, and incarceration.

For example, it found that 62 percent of drug offenders admitted to state prisons were black, 13 times the rate of white men. Black men are incarcerated almost 10 times the rate of white men. For men over the age of 18, it reported that one in 20 black men is in a state or federal prison, whereas one in 180 white men are incarcerated.

The report found such racial disparities to exist throughout the United States, and they were even larger in some states than others. It claims that equal protection before the law must be addressed, and it made key recommendations to help correct these human rights violations. The recommendations include, "repeal of mandatory minimum sentences for drug offenders; increase the availability of alternative sanctions: eliminate different sentencing structures for powder cocaine and crack cocaine; increase the use of drug courts: increase the availability of substance abuse treatment; eliminate racial profiling; require police to keep and make public statistics on the race of arrested drug offenders and the location of the arrests."

Amnesty International Report: 1999

Amnesty International USA finds many Human Rights violations in America's Penal System:

In October, 1999, Amnesty International (AI) turned its attention to human rights violations in the United States, publishing a 150-page report, *USA: Rights for All*. Along with focussing on such topics as police brutality, the death penalty, arms trading, and detention of asylum-seekers, AI took a look at the treatment of prisoners in America's prisons.

Although AI has not come out to condemn the US Drug War for its role in the rise of the prison population, it has noted that the number of inmates has more than tripled and the number of women inmates has quadrupled since 1980. It noted serious complaints of abuse and poor conditions by inmates held in privately run institutions.

The report found many complaints of sexual and physical abuse in the prisons. Some prisoners fear retaliation or are too vulnerable to complain about rape and sexual abuse in their institutions. There were concerns that "staff of the opposite sex are allowed to undertake in searches that involve body contact and to be present where inmates are naked." Some restraining techniques were found to be "cruel, inhuman and sometimes life-threatening." Use of restraint chairs, chemical sprays, and electro-shock devices such as stun belts continue, despite their being banned in other countries due to the pain and health risks involved. In addition, pregnant women complain of routine shackling.

The increasing number of inmates sentenced to "supermax" prisons was a concern to AI. The units in such prisons are designed for long-term isolation of dangerous or disruptive prisoners, but their concrete and steel construction and confinement to cells for 23 or more hours per day result in "cruel, inhuman or degrading treatment or punishment."

In many facilities, health care is inadequate, AI reports. "Complaints include grossly deficient treatment for the mentally ill; lack of provision for women's health needs; failing to deliver prescribed drugs; and refusing or delaying necessary medical treatment...Lack of proper screening for communicable diseases combined with overcrowded and insanitary conditions are putting many lives at serious and unnecessary risk."

Hopefully, these findings will trigger a deeper look into the allegations made in this important report. AI has called for independent agencies to monitor the conditions and to find remedies for these abuses that will bring the US government into compliance with international standards guaranteeing human rights for all, including those who are in prisons and jails. For more information, please visit their website at www.amnestyusa.org/rightsforall/.

For more personal stories and photos, as well as other useful information visit the Human Rights and the Drug War website:

www.hr95.org

PO Box 1716, El Cerrito CA 94530

Call for a Drug War Truce

Preamble: No civilized nation makes war on its own citizens. We, the People, did not declare war on our government, nor do we wish to fight its Drug War.

Hence, we now petition for redress of grievances, as follows:

Whereas any just government derives its authority from a respect of the People's rights and powers; and

Whereas the US government has resorted to unilateral military force in the Drug War without making any good faith effort to negotiate a peace settlement;

Therefore, We hereby call for a Drug War Truce during which to engage our communities and governments in peace negotiations, under the following terms:

Article 1: The US shall withdraw from, repudiate, or amend any and all international Treaties or agreements limiting its ability to alter domestic drug policy.

Article 2: No patient shall be prosecuted nor any health care professional penalized for possession or use of any mutually agreed upon medications.

Article 3: Drug policy shall henceforth protect all fundamental rights, as described below:

1. Each person retains all their inalienable Constitutional and Human Rights, without exception. No drug regulation shall violate these Rights.

2. The benefit of the doubt shall always be given to the accused and to any property or assets at risk. Courts shall allow the accused to present directly to the jury any defense based on these Rights, any explanation of motive, or any mitigating circumstances, such as religion, culture, or necessity.

3. No victim: no crime. The burden of proof and corroboration in all proceedings shall lie with the government. No secret witness nor paid participatory testimony shall be permitted in court, including that of any government agent or informant who stands to materially gain through the disposition of a drug case or forfeited property. No civil asset forfeiture shall be levied against a family home or legitimate means of commercial livelihood.

4. Issues of entrapment, government motive, and official misconduct shall all be heard by the jury in any drug case, civil or criminal. Government agents who violate the law are fully accountable and shall be prosecuted accordingly.

5. Mandatory minimum sentences undermine our system of justice. The jury shall be informed of all penalties attached to any

offense before deliberating a verdict. Courts shall have discretion to reduce penalties in the interest of justice.

Article 4: We propose a Drug War Truce and call for the immediate release of all non-violent and, aside from drug charges involving adults only, law-abiding citizens.

Article 5: No non-violent drug charges involving adults only shall be enforced or prosecuted until all parties have agreed to, and implemented, a drug policy based on full respect for fundamental Rights and personal responsibility.

Fill out and mail to:

FCDA / Family Council on Drug Awareness
PO Box 1716
El Cerrito CA 94530

Signature: _____

Name: _____

Address: _____

_____

Phone: _____

Internet: _____

UN Treaties on Human Rights

The UN Universal Declaration of Human Rights (UDHR) is an international agreement, but it is not a treaty, and therefore is not directly enforceable under the US Constitution.

However, many of its principles are written into legally binding treaties, such as the *International Covenant on Civil and Political Rights*, the *Convention on the Elimination of All Forms of Racial Discrimination*, the *Convention Against Torture and Other Cruel, Inhuman or Degrading Treatment*, and the *Convention on the Prevention and Punishment of the Crime of Genocide*.

For a full set of international treaties on human rights law, contact:

The Human Rights Reporting Project
Meikljohn Civil Liberties Institute
PO Box 673, Berkeley CA 94701-0673
Phone: 510-848-0599, Fax: 510-848-6008, Email: mcli@igc.org

Useful Internet Sites and Resources

**American Civil
Liberties Union**
125 Broad St. 18th
Floor
NYC, NY 10004-2400
212-344-3005
www.aclu.org

Amnesty International
322 Eighth Ave.
New York NY 10001
212-807-8400
www.amnestyusa.org

**Common Sense for
Drug Policy**
3220 N St. NW #141
Washington DC 20007
Phone: 703-354-5694
www.csdp.org

**Criminal Justice
Policy Foundation**
1225 "I" St. NW # 500
Washington DC 20005
202-312-2015
www.cjpf.org

**Drug Reform
Coordination Network**
2000 P. St. NW # 210
Washington DC 20036
202-293-8340
www.drcnet.org ,
www.druglibrary.org

**Families Against
Mandatory Minimums**
1612 K St. # 1400
Washington DC 20006
202-822-6700
www.famm.org

**Family Council on
Drug Awareness**
PO Box 1716
El Cerrito, CA 94530
www.fcda.org

**Forfeiture Endangers
American Rights**
PO Box 339855
Washington DC
20033-3985
888-FEAR-001
www.fear.org

**Human Rights and
the Drug War**
PO Box 1716
El Cerrito, CA 94530
510-215-8326
www.hr95.org

Human Rights Watch
350 Fifth Ave. 34th
Floor
NYC, NY 10118-3299
212-290-4700
www.hrw.org

**Justice Policy Institute
/Center on Juvenile
and Criminal Justice**
1622 Folsom Street
San Francisco CA
94103 / 415-621-5661
www.cjcj.org

1234 Massachusetts
Ave. NW # C-1009
Washington DC 20005
202-737-7270

**The Lindesmith
Center- Drug Policy
Foundation**
925 Ninth Avenue,

New York NY 10019
212-548-0695
www.lindesmith.org,
www.dpf.org

**Marijuana Policy
Project**
PO Box 77492, Capitol
Hill
Washington DC 20013
202-462-5747
www.mpp.org

**Media Awareness
Project/ Drug Sense**
PO Box 651
Porterville CA 93258
800-266-5759
www.mapinc.org/
www.drugsense.org

**National Organization
to Reform Marijuana
Laws (NORML)**
1001 Connecticut Ave.,
710
Washington DC 20036
202-483-5500
www.norml.org

**The November
Coalition / TNC**
795 South Cedar
Colville WA 99114
509-684-1550
www.november.org

Sentencing Project
514 Tenth St. NW
1000
Washington DC 20004
202-628-0871
www.sentencingproject.
org

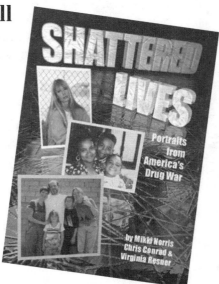